Printing error

Please note that the 1st prize poem on page 25 "The s
was submitted as four lines per verse i.e a total of 20 l
The error came in producing the book for printing beca
The submitted poem reads:

CU00950586

As I've wandered through life's mazes, I've se
I've seen many cruel winters turn into gentle s
Nothing stays the same as I pass along the wa
And the stars are getting older every day.

There was bombing all around me in the season of my birth,
And still they drop on other lands on Earth.
Will they ever cease? Can anybody say?
And the stars are getting older every day.

Things have happened through our time in ways we never could conceive,
So very much has changed in ways we can't believe.
Nothing that we see around is ever here to stay,
And the stars are getting older every day.

But our lives are just an instant in the vast expanse of time,
Where mountain ranges disappear and climb.
Majestic peaks are crumbling into tiny lumps of clay,
And the stars are getting older every day.

Will the changes that we see around last out until eternity?
Will there come a time when all change will cease to be?
And in the distant future will all ages fade away?
Or will the stars keep getting older every day?

SALTFORD FESTIVAL

2017

POETRY COMPETITION

CONTENTS

Winner of the First Prize

George Liddell "The stars are getting older every day" page 25

Winner of the Second Prize

Dominic Lopez-Real "The Tortoise Dream" page 34.

20. The Sock thief	Anne Eastaugh
38. Ode to a Bus Stop	Malcolm Guthrie
39. View from the Round Hill	Malcolm Guthrie
16. Begin Again	Rebecca Hilton
24. Welcome to the World	George Liddell
25. The stars are getting older every day	**George Liddell 1st Prize**
26. I'll cherish this moment	George Liddell
34. The Tortoise Dream	**Dominic Lopez-Real 2nd Prize**
35. My Dancing Elephant	Dominic Lopez-Real
36. How to become a fossil	Dominic Lopez-Real
29. Chakras of Mother Earth	Dawn Minall
30. Cloak of Black	Dawn Minall
31. Dawn	Dawn Minall
32. A South Westerly	Dawn Minall
33. Yellow Beacon	Dawn Minall
42. strange Season	Tony Mitchell
43. Crowning Glory	Tony Mitchell
41. Valentine Rose	Martin Parsons
12. Eyes to See	Winifred Rickard
13. To Concorde	Winifred Rickard
14. Musings on Saltford Weir	Winifred Rickard
15. OMG (Just a thought)	Winifred Rickard
6. 2 am	George Shiel
17. The Abbey Ruins	Wendy Tyrell
37. Tiger Poem	Abigail Watson-Gover (9 years old)
50. The clock stands still just short of 12	Jill Williams

ENTRY RULES FOR THE COMPETITION

The poem must have no more than 20 lines and be on any theme

1st Prize £20   2nd Prize   £10

Entry Fee £2 per poem and multiple entries permitted

There were three qualified judges who marked out of 20 basing their markings on:

Enjoyment, Content (interest) and Quality of writing

The winners were the two with the highest combined marks from all three judges

The judges decision is final

Prizes are presented at the Opening Day of the Festival, June 10th 2017

Prizes are also given to the two entries from young people

All authors and other interested people are invited to hear readings of the poems at a meeting on Friday, June 16th 10.30-12 noon at the Saltford Library

'2 am' by George Shiel

Patrolling the darkness

Pulse racing.

Breathing the night air.

Streetlight moths

Smelling the sweetness,

Of a stranger's cigarette.

Eyed up as I pass.

Judged no threat.

Pacing faster,

No one around now,

Needing to get back,

Stayed out too long.

Family waiting,

Safety and warmth there.

Keys in the lock

And I'm where I belong.

I love oranges by June Barclay

I thought I'd pen a little rhyme
about my fruit bowl filled with lime
and tasty things like pear and apple.
Then came a problem I'd to grapple.

Lots of words rhyme with banana
Like iguana and sultana.
Words rhyme with lemon, grape and berry
but with 'orange' – none! Not <u>many.</u>

Words rhyme with fruits like clementine,
satsumas and with tangerine -
all cousins of the orange thing
that does not rhyme with anything.

Apricot and even cherry
Rhyme with yacht and loganberry.
There's rhymes for lots of other words,
but not for 'orange' – how absurd.

So in the end I've had to cool it
with my fruit bowl rhyming couplet.
My search for rhymes with 'orange' saught,
have completely come to naught.

A Love Story by June Barclay

My heart was yours from that first nervous meeting at the dance

"I love the shine the disco ball casts on your chestnut hair."

My insides pounded, I hoped you'd walk me to the bus stance.

I   *wanted to walk you home, for us to become a pair.*

We walked and talked and loved and laughed and loved some more and planned.

I loved your chestnut curls shining beneath your bridal veil

My heart burst as you placed the ring, and then you took my hand.

That day we made our lifelong vows and you became my girl.

We loved, we laughed, we made a home and then we bought a cot.

I loved your damp and straggly hair when finally you cried.

I'd tried, and we were almost three – but two would be our lot.

You laid your mop of curls upon my chest. We sadly sighed.

Time went by, we laughed again and I loved you even more.

I loved the shine upon your hair when we both turned silver.

I just recall our first meeting on that disco dance floor.

I now sit and remind you of our first dance together.

Slowly I'm forgetting stuff and fear things that aren't there.

I love your thinning, greying hair, not shining and un-brushed.

Now kiss goodbye to me, your girl with shining chestnut hair.

I am left the only one that recalls when we were us.

Leaving Ireland by June Barclay

The ship moved away from the docks.
Tears flowed, handkerchiefs waved.
Sad women wore hats and best frocks
The men grave, still - as men must behave.

Tears flowed, handkerchiefs waved.
Thoughts of the past filled every mind
The men grave, still - the way men must behave
Leaving famine and family behind.

Thoughts of the past filled every mind
Their new futures filled each with great fear
Leaving famine and family behind
They were losing the lives they held dear.

Their new futures filled each with great fear.
Sad women wore hats and best frocks
They were losing the lives they held dear.
The ship moved away from the docks.

I am a Metaphor by Rebecca Bryce

I am a metaphor – or so they all tell me

I'm a gullible kitten, I'm as fragile as Ming

I think like an idiot at times during panic

And act like a child of four on a swing

My age is a staircase I'm adverse to climbing

My past is a dream – it's all gone in a haze

I don't think my thoughts can be measured in timing

For I am a metaphor – A mouse in a maze

They tell me I'm human but act like an alien

They ask me what planet I've blown in from

I don't mind their comments – I find them endearing

For I am a metaphor –it's where I belong

Just somebody I used to know ....by Rebecca Bryce

We screamed like children in sheer delight

Scooping up bright coloured sea urchin shells

Playing at being The Famous Five

Enjoying the Now and feeling alive

We two 20 something girls

I cried on her shoulder, and she on mine

When life got tough for us both at times

One husband leaves, the other won't go

But we had our friendship and let that grow

We two 40 something girls

I think of those moments sometimes in a haze

She's no longer part of my life these sad days

Caught in the midst of a spiteful plan

Hatched by a jealous so-called friend

Two lost 60 something girls

EYES TO SEE by Winifred Rickard

I've met Jesus often today

In people I've met on the way.

There was one who gave me a smile

And one who walked the extra mile,

One who gave her time to listen

Whose sad eyes with tears did glisten.

Another who said a short prayer

Giving me time to stand and stare.

And one I met so full of need

To whom I gave much loving need.

Someone new I did discover

As we learnt more of each other,

Of intellect taking measure

And in mind games finding pleasure.

Best of all there was one so kind

Whose safe love was easy to find.

So what the Bible says is true,

God's spirit lives in me and you.

TO CONCORDE by Winifred Rickard

Beautiful bird, you scythed the skies,

Blasting your trail through the blue.

We couldn't help but raise our eyes

And our hearts were lifted too.

You were one of science's joys

An engineering wonder,

Biggest and best of big boys' toys.

Your engines roared like thunder.

Concorde, in our hearts you will live

We raise our glasses to you,

Your supersonic spirit give

To sunshine's shimmer as you flew.

MUSINGS ON SALTFORD WEIR by Winifred Rickard

Like a still river

Into the weir bursts forth

Faster than any man-made speed

Or a rocket's thrust

Through starry galaxies

The climax of man's spiritual need.

Currents hidden lie

In places dark and deep.

Anger underneath is boiling

Moving t'wards the weir.

In freedom now released

Mighty swirls and eddies coiling.

Sadness slowly flows

Within the sludge and silt,

Still moving t'wards the mighty weir

Sediments of time

Particles of much grief

Bursting forth in tear upon tear.

OMG (Just a thought)

by

Winifred Rickard

OMG, the people say,

OMG, the people pray,

But are we His anyway?

BEGIN AGAIN by Rebecca Hilton

Still we scratch the last bite marks of cool solstice.

Sensibly boarding together. to vail the overcast.

A gentle beast's breath gathers against the windows.

    taming our seamless picture.

Away with the film by the passing of an early March coat

Once more. warm life adapts to seasonal change

    Without question.

    with some complaint..

The gold leaf in our eyes crumbles to become Earth's

    acquaintance.

We awaken. to the surprise of the bloom reoccurring.

    as a curling yellow flame.

The Abbey Ruins by Wendy Tyrell

Alone I stand, yet not alone
The breeze blows gently around the abbey ruins hewn in stone

Ghosts of monks linger here
Can you not feel them in this sacred space once held dear?

A house of Austin Canons was founded by an earl
By a tranquil Keynsham riverside in memory of a son, who died

Men of god once dwelt here in obedience and in prayer
A black robed band of brothers secure in their abbot's care

300 years and more it stood, an abbey of some renown
Until for love, a petulant king brought religion tumbling down

Desecration and sorrow swept England's holy land
Monastic life dissolved, destroyed by King Henry's royal hand

Our abbey walls have disappeared
The stones helped build a road that pollutes the air of this
sacred space where men of God once trode

Keynsham Abbey founded 1166
Last Abbot John Staunton and 10 monks surrendered Abbey 23.1.1539

DANCING IN THE RAIN by Anne Eastaugh

I'm dancing in the rain,

I don't care about how wet I'll get,

Stamping in the puddles

Kicking up a storm,

Swaying to and fro

First the path and then the lane

I'm 84 today and I don't mind

If you think I'm mad!

I'm dancing in the rain.

Wrapped up well in mac and wellies

The rain is bouncing off the path

And running down the drain.

Today I'm well and in my prime

Tomorrow may be different

Then I will stay indoors

And watch the world go by.

THE BUILDING SITE by Anne Eastaugh

The Building Site,

Cranes Hoisting, lifting, diggers digging

Concrete poured, paths are laid

A giant puzzle with pieces missing.

People peering through a hole in the fence

Is it flats or houses or a shop?

Looks a proper mess to me one man said

Men's boots and clothes caked in mud, hard hats on head.

An older man lifts his grandson to see

The work being done

Grandad said I bet those bricks weigh a ton!

The little boy points, Look Grandad a digger and a crane.

Another delivery arrives at the site

The lorry moves slowly, the space is tight

It drops its load inside the gate

It's nearly time to go home, he's nearly too late.

All is silent at the site

Men have gone home for tea

No more lorries or trucks carrying loads

Until tomorrow this is a quiet road.

THE SOCK THIEF by Anne Eastaugh

The Sock thief has been at it again!

The washer has finished

I'm sure I put 4 pairs in

But only 3 pairs came out

And 1 lonely sock all alone

The sock drawer will diminish

I peer in the drum to no avail

It has gone. walked up the lane

To find happy sock heaven.

MOTHER EARTH by Hayley Bond

I, Mother earth, stand on the brink of my destruction,

I see my once-harmless children grow into spiteful,

heartless monsters, trying to destroy me, get rid of me forever,

trying to blank me out of their lives.

I hear my fascinating pets begging for their magnificent homes

back, pleading for their so-called friends to stop.

I smell the disgusting fumes coming out of those

dreadful machines - otherwise known as cars -

attempting to make my once luxurious life a misery.

I feel betrayed and disrespected, like a toy that had

been discarded by it's ungrateful owner,

I am a story that never got told.

I feel, I smell, I hear, I see these depressing things

I wait for my death to come.

I gave you a life, a home, a family,

Why do you disrespect me?   Aged 11 years

21

SHOWER THEM by Hayley Bond

Shower them with presents

Shower them with love

Shower them with flowers

Tell all the Gods above.

Give them a teddy bear

Give them a card

Give them your heart

Cause you love them real hard.

Tell them that you love them

Tell them that you care

Tell them that they're special

Cause love is in the air.

Aged 11 years

MY GRANDMOTHER by Hayley Bond

Bread pudding maker

Beauty complimenter

Lipstick applier

My grandmother

Aged 11 years

WELCOME TO THE WORLD by George Liddell

Welcome to the world little baby,
Come on in little man,
A miracle now has unfolded,
Another new life now began.

I'm sorry that it's all so chaotic,
That it's not such a perfect place,
I'm afraid that we've been so neglectful,
What we've done to it is a disgrace.

Well at times we did make an effort,
And maybe we had some success.
Maybe there's some little thing that we did,
That did not add to the mess.
I'll watch you grow up and I'll help you,
But some day I'm afraid we must part,
And hope that when that day comes between us,
I'll have helped you make a good start.

I know that you're weak and you're helpless,
My tiny, wee Little-Boy-Blue,
But grow up in strength and in wisdom,
For someday it will be up to you.

The Stars Are Getting Older Every Day by George Liddell

As I've wandered through life's mazes,
I've seen many wondrous things,
I've seen many cruel winters turn into gentle springs,
Nothing stays the same as I pass along the way,
And the stars are getting older every day.

There was bombing all around me
In the season of my birth,
And still they drop on other lands on Earth.
Will they ever cease? Can anybody say?
And the stars are getting older every day.

Things have happened through our time,
In ways we never could conceive,
So very much has changed in ways we can't believe.
Nothing that we see around is ever here to stay,
And the stars are getting older every day.

But our lives are just an instant
In the vast expanse of time,
Where mountain ranges disappear and climb.
Majestic peaks are crumbling into tiny lumps of clay,
And the stars are getting older every day.

Will the changes that we see around
Last out until eternity?
Will there come a time when change will cease to be?
And in the distant future will all ages fade away?
Or will the stars keep getting older every day?

I'll Cherish this Moment by George Liddell

I'll cherish this moment the rest of my life;
This moment when I am with you.
Though ages shall roll, I will never forget,
And I'll cherish this moment anew.

> Though miles are between us and ever will be,
> I'll cherish that time our paths crossed
> As we sailed on life's sea on our separate ways
> And briefly together were tossed.

I'll cherish this moment the rest of my life;
This moment when I am with you.
Though ages shall roll, I will never forget,
And I'll cherish this moment anew.

> Through sunshine and storms I will travel along,
> Whatever tomorrow will bring,
> But deep in my memory this moment shall last,
> Forever that magic will cling.

I'll cherish this moment the rest of my life;
This moment when I am with you.
Though ages shall roll, I will never forget,
And I'll cherish this moment anew.

PRIDE COMES BEFORE A FALL by David Cox

Once there lived a might king

Who wished to hear the people sing

In praise of him and him alone

As he sat upon his golden throne.

The king was Ozymandias

The roof of whose palace was sparkling brass

So vain he was and very proud

He thought of a way to impress the crowd.

He decided to build a statue high

A magnificent one that would reach to the sky

A statue of Ozymandias

The roof of whose palace was made of brass.

The head he thought was the important part,

So this he made, just for a start

In gold so pure it glowed in the sun.

"This head" he said "is a magnificent one".

When he came to the feet of his statue gay he made its feet from the local clay,

When the rains poured down they washed away the feet of his statue made of clay

So we can learn from this stupid king that outward show's not the greatest thing!

That without foundations firm & sound our lives tumble worthless to the ground!

IN BETWEEN by David Cox

The dirt and grime, the sludge and slime

Are left behind.

The smoking chimneys of the growling town

have disappeared behind the grassy folds of sleeping hills.

The stillness of the sunlit countryside

Is broken only by the happy lapping

Of the water on our sides;

And the steady muffled plod as Dobbin, sturdy in his shaggy coat

Strains onward with his heavy load.

The still clear water lights up with reds and blues

with brilliant hues of yellow roses

Heap on heap of glossy posies

Reflected from our floating home,

And then are gone;

But Nature has not been unkind,

And with a sparkling cloak

Has clothed the countryside we pass in colours which

Outstrip the brilliant paint of boat and barge.

Until again the rumbling clouds of clinging smoke pollute and spoil

her handiwork.

FROM BRISTOL TO BATH ALONG THE AVON.

CHAKRAS OF MOTHER EARTH by Dawn Minall

Iridescent colours arc across the stormy skies,

The chakras of Mother Nature.

Linking us through colour,

Pulsating through our cells.

A perfect portal in the sky,

Helping us to connect.

The grey skies and the rain,

Reflect our tears and fears.

Glimpses of sunshine, however brief,

Reflect our joy and laughter.

Our DNA is linked;

Together we hold the future,

For future generations.

CLOAK OF BLACK by Dawn Minall

In his cloak of black,

He defends his territory.

Strutting his stuff,

The dominant male.

Guarding his partner and offspring,

Against other marauding males.

All under cloud cover.

And then the sun comes out.

His feathers no longer, shiny black,

But purple and blue and green.

A hint of burgundy as well.

Iridescent, sparkly, beautiful,

Reflecting the rays of sunlight.

His extended tail feathers

Wave in the breeze.

A truly magnificent sight.

DAWN by Dawn Minall

Dawn, the chorus
Sunrise lighting up the sky.
Shadows retreating,
To reveal a living landscape.
A time of quiet,
To look and listen.
Meditation time.
Lose yourself,
Connect to centre,
Until the sun is high in the sky.
Wrap up the silence
Within your soul,
Until tomorrow's dawn.

.

A SOUTH WESTERLY by Dawn Minall

Bringing weather from warmer climes,

The wind is whistling past.

The trees are bending over.

My waistcoat fills, expanding out.

A ringer for the Michelin Man.

Lightly built, not much resistance,

My feet are lifted off the ground.

I'm flying, I'm really flying.

Just because I can.

YELLOW BEACON by Dawn Minall

Your trumpeting heads,

Standing aloft on tubular stems

Proud, defiant, glorious.

Defying winters' chilly blasts.

Vibrant yellow, imitating sunshine,

Paler hues, tempering.

Deep orange cutting through,

The darker shades of gloom.

A beacon to attract us.

You stir up our emotions,

You raise our soul vibrations.

THE TORTOISE'S DREAM by Dominic Lopez-Real

I'm really fed up with this house on my back.

I can't run, I can't jump, I just plod, and that's that.

Do you know what I'd do if this shell wasn't here?

I'd race round the zoo. I'd shout and I'd cheer.

I'd swing with the monkeys and steal their bananas,

then dive in the lake and fight the piranhas.

I'd pinch all the sweets from the kids in the playground,

then tickle the Lions and escape like a greyhound.

I'd be going so fast you'd see fire and steam!

Now I know what you're thinking - it's all just a dream.

But it's true! I could be like a speedy gazelle,

if only my mum would get rid of this shell……….

MY DANCING ELEPHANT by Dominic Lopez-Real

When I was young, I spent a week

with relatives in Delhi.

And I brought back a special pet:

a singing, dancing Ellie!

She would waltz around the garden

and foxtrot on the path.

Samba in the dining room

and tap dance in the bath.

I even saw her doing ballet

in a launderette.

and boy I tell you, she could do

a perfect pirouette.

I didn't keep her very long.

(Mum said she was smelly)

But now she's really famous in

"Come Dancing" on the telly.

HOW TO BECOME A FOSSIL by Dominic Lopez -Real

How to become a fossil, in three easy steps:

One: you need good bones. So eat your cheddar cheese,
and visit the dentist. Twice a year please.

Two: You need a sudden end. Perhaps a flood,
and then make sure you're buried in some mud.

Three: lie still a million years. This won't be quick.
A "do not disturb" sign might do the trick.

Then if you're lucky, you'll be highly prized,
because my friend, you will be fossilized!

<u>TIGER POEM by Abigail Watson-Gove</u>

Tiger, tiger in the cage, slowly building up with rage,

I can see your eyes so bright, never fading in the night.

If you could, I bet you would, go to your parents in the wood.

Then they would come, with their rum, the male humans

unwelcome.

Would you pounce, or would you flee?

For that part is not up to me.

Though with the pounce I would disagree, because imagine if
that was me and it would be a big mistake, for it would be a
piece of cake.

For those humans may have knives, illegal and sharp to
terrorise those beautiful never fading eyes.

Aged 9 years

ODE TO A BUS STOP BY MALCOLM GUTHRIE

ON X39, ON X39, FURNISHED AND BURNISHED

BY BATH'S WINTER SUN.

THE MONEY IS SPENT NOW, THE BAGS WE HAVE

PROVE IT AND 'COME BACK AGAIN' IS THE

MESSAGE WE'RE LEFT WITH.

WE'RE NEARLY HOME NOW, A PRESS ON

THE BUTTON, A JUDDERING STOP AND WITH

THANKS TO THE DRIVER, WE MAKE OUR DEPARTURE.

WITH GOODS CLUTCHED BEFORE US AND

WITH POWER IN OUR FINGERTIP, THE TRAFFIC

IS HALTED AND A LITTLE GREEN MAN,

BIDS US CROSS NOW IN SAFETY.

THE KETTLE IS ON NOW, THE FIRESIDE

IS CALLING AND EASTER IS WITH US, SO

GIVE THANKS THAT WE MADE IT.

With apologies to Sir John Betjeman and Miss Joan Hunter Dunn.

38

VIEW FROM THE ROUND HILL by Malcolm Guthrie

It's an hour from Home and Garden

It's hard work across the fields

At the road there's great temptation

But the Inn must needs to wait.

The lane keeps getting steeper

And one's age begins to tell

A breather on the lower slope is gratefully received

Before the summit's last long climb.

Permissive Path it's labelled as our legs begin to find

And a well-worn bench is welcomed

As the thermos flask is used

But this is God's own Country and our eyes can see His work.

To the north we have the Malverns

To the south a whitened horse

To the East a Georgian City

But the west has our own village with our loved ones in its care

So what is that which moves us after all the breathless climb?

Well, give thanks a Sunday service when it's time for silent prayer.

For we are only short time servants in a World that needs our care.

THE RIVER AVON by Enid Bryant

I spring from Acton Turville village,

And gently flow towards the Cotswold Ridge.

I hurry over twenty hills,

But slow my pace beneath Bradford Bridge.

Winding on from Glos. And Wilts., I sally

Into Somerset. I carve the landscape in the vale,

Adorn myself with week and weeping willow,

And welcome tarmac road and iron rail.

At Pulteney Bridge I plunge above the weir,

And all my living creatures whirl around.

Further on, by grassy bank, I then proceed;

Jewels shining on my back; birdsong the only sound.

I leave behind the elegance of stone,

And join Kennet Canal, my little cousin.

Then off I gurgle, sturgid, slow and dirty.

Maybe I'll flood awhile, the effluent my reason.

At Saltford, I smile, bob little boats on the Marina.

The 'Jolly Sailor' beckons, but my water's in a spate.

Helpless, I'm rushing past these tempting beauties

To the deepest Gorge; to the towering Bridge. TOWARDS MY FATE.

Valentine Rose

By martin Parsons

The faded rose
Lies in the gutter
A gentle breeze
Petals flutter
That's the way
Some love goes
Like a blackbird
In its' death throes

STRANGE SEASON – by Tony Mitchell

in the style of the poets of Old England, before the Normans came.

Winter sun,   world-warming;

Leaf crackle,   crisp air, colourful,

Swishing underfoot,   dying.

Cold nip on   numb fingers,

Frost fiend   forever threatening life

Chill chasing chill,   till we choose heat.

Fire crackles well,   wood spit warming us

Fearful, fur full,   Feast Hall hot,

As trees drop leaves,   colour-carpeting paths.

Silvered lattice work   glitters in sunlight.

Eye level   light blinds

Breath smokes   but beauty abounds,

Doom laden   but lovely.

No hint of new life   till years change.

CROWNING GLORY by Tony Mitchell

See how the hairs grow gold,
Glow, stare, crack then fall.
Old strands lack light,
Look thin, not rich and full.

Rapunzel rolled and twisted,
Turned the tower down
Dropped locks; but only
Youth could surge, spawn

Growth like this. Years drag
The life out, pale and poised
For death, and dwindle
Into deserts without end, raised

Mounds, dry brittle sticks,
Too frail, a careworn crucifix.

See Webb, E., The Plays of Samuel Beckett, p 33
Beckett, S., Waiting for Godot, pp 52, 62 (paper back, 1973)

Writing Poetry by Julia Coombe

I write poetry because it revives the soul

It sprinkles me with something fresh

Like the pat, patter, pat of the rain

Gently, gently it revives the fluffy mind

Thank you the flower will sing

As the first crocus heralding spring

The little prince of an amber crown

Will raise its little head above the ground

To the pearly drip, drop of the rain

Saying, now it can live again -

And again

It is revived

Eventide by Julia Coombe

It is blowing in the wind,

the candle is blowing in the wind.

If we were to carry it, in our hand,

as a precious gift, as a light to lighten.

As a light that must not go out.

Like a candle, blowing in the wind,

his white robe, is blowing in the wind.

The daisy has shut her face, for it is eventide,

then again, tomorrow, it will awaken.

But how many morrows will there be?

To the one of homespun creed,

the doors will surely open.

To the seed that fell into the ground,

such fruit will surely be born.

But what of us, what is our creed?

HOVERING ON THE WATER by Julia Coombe

hovering, shimmering, shivering, upon the water
in a watery mysterious non being world
without land
without trees
without sky
without stars
without a day
and without night.

Hovering and shimmering and moving along,
was God freely in a land of chaos.
Then a thought occurred to him,
watery and a bit unfamiliar.

So he said,
let there be something,
can't think what?
I know,
light!

And it was.

Inspired by Luke 2 22-38 by Julia Coombe

She burnt her life right through,
She was an good woman, old and true,
She was a candle burning brightly,
She was a promise to come rightly.
Anna at the temple, counted.

A shouting some may be,
A praising sounds good to me,
A jumping could be fun,
But a marching has been done.
Some may be exclaiming,
Some may be a hopping,
A dancing could give me joy.
But I am just a counting, a counting,
Till the day I see my boy.

So turning, burning candle brightly,
Turn your life right through.
What else does a candle do?
Anna, was an old woman, good and true,
She burned her life right through.

An Impression in October by Julia Coombe

Pink fluffy clouds

To match the roses

Dancing in the breeze

Like confetti

Autumn rose

(The one I love so much)

Little black cat

Sharpening his paws

Against the tree

(The tree we planted carefully)

To match the roses

Amber fruit now dancing too

Gifts that are free

So pretty is the little black cat

Dragonfly Days by Helen Crew

Wasps dive in fizzy drinks,

sun oil spills and slips through cracks in parched lawns-

dragonfly days.

Acres of canvas in campsites with dew-drenched dawns,

dragonfly days.

Greenhouses heavy with tomato scent,

Heat from sticky tarmac seeps through flip flops-

Dragonfly days.

Ice-cream van tunes, melting lollipops,

Dragonfly days.

Kids playing with hosepipes,

Caravans crawling though country lanes-

Dragonfly days.

As Autumn approaches, all that remains,

memories of dragonfly days.

The Clock stands still just short of twelve

By Jill Williams

The village rises gently from the river, cottages staggering, unevenly up the slope share evidence of time past.

A deep, wide fireplace, a well, long dry, part worn flagstones hewn from local stone once laid to last.

The summer sun warms the pale limestone walls that flank the village street and lead upwards to the square.

The church tucked modestly in the shadow of the pine trees lies near the resolute, ancient Manor - oh for conversation from this pair!

What lies beneath the soil is, at times, revealed. Great fossil mollusks lying coiled, serpent like, embedded in the rock

Some wrenched from their resting places are built into a more recent limestone landscape, to be marveled at by passers by.

The light footprint of the Romans has offered only a coffin, coins and shards.

In my own garden I often marvel at patterned fragments of blue ceramic and tiny tubes and bowls of clay pipes smoked by Victorian owners of my home.

How many years has the clock stood still and what will be found to represent the detritus of our time?

Made in the USA
Columbia, SC
08 June 2017